Flushed

By Catherine Cranfield

Published by Playdead Press 2021

© Catherine Cranfield 2021

Catherine Cranfield has asserted her rights under the Copyright, Design and Patents Act, 1988, to be identified as the author of this work.

A CIP catalogue record for this book is available from the British Library.

ISBN 978-1-910067-94-9

Caution

All rights whatsoever in this play are strictly reserved and application for performance should be sought through the author before rehearsals begin. No performance may be given unless a license has been obtained.

This book is sold subject to the condition that it shall not by way of trade or otherwise, be lent, resold, hired out, or otherwise circulated without the publisher's prior consent in any form of binding or cover other than that in which it is published and without a similar condition including this condition being imposed on the subsequent purchaser.

Playdead Press
www.playdeadpress.com

This version of the script is in accordance with the 2021 performance of **FLUSHED** at Park Theatre, which was presented as part of the *Say It, Women!* double bill, featuring two untold stories celebrating women's strength.

This run of **FLUSHED** was a co-production between **Theatre Unlocked** and **Grace Dickson Productions**, presented in association with **Park Theatre**.

The cast and creative team were as follows:

MARNIE	Elizabeth Hammerton
JEN	Iona Champain
Writer & Director	Catherine Cranfield
Executive Producer	Elis Shotton
Associate Producer	Grace Dickson
Stage Manager	Alice Wood
Sound Design	Oscar Maguire
Lighting Design	Anthony Englezou

Supported using public funding by Arts Council England

FLUSHED was first performed in 2018 at 53two in Manchester, where it was the first production to be supported by their 'FOUNDation' award. The cast and creative team were as follows:

MARNIE	Georgia Dawson
JEN	Harriet Rose Millsopp
Writer & Director	Catherine Cranfield
Producer	Elis Shotton
Assistant Director	Antonia Ward

FLUSHED has since been staged at multiple theatres, including Underbelly at the 2018 Edinburgh Fringe, and Barbican Centre as part of Fertility Fest 2019. The cast and crew for these performances include:

MARNIE	Georgia Dawson
JEN	Iona Champain
Writer & Director	Catherine Cranfield
Producer	Elis Shotton
Assistant Director	Phoebe Gibby
Assistant Producer	Rose de Castellane

Special thanks go to:
Park Theatre, Mobius Industries, Arts Council England, Simon Naylor, Alexandra Maxwell, Dave Howell, Tracey Woolley, Jessica Hepburn, Gabby Vautier, Segun Olaiya, Peter James CBE, Alice Packham, Jack Donald, Guillaume Doussin, Lidia Crisafulli, Underbelly Edinburgh, Lyric Hammersmith, Chelsea and Westminster Hospital, The Daisy Network (in particular, Marie Gerval, Kate Maclaran, Amy Bennie), all the women who were generous enough to share their experiences of POI, Jane and Michael Cranfield for their consistent support and endless ferrying of toilets.

About Park Theatre

Park Theatre was founded by Artistic Director, Jez Bond and Creative Director Emeritus, Melli Marie. The building opened in May 2013 and, with four West End transfers, two National Theatre transfers and 13 national tours in its first eight years, quickly garnered a reputation as a key player in the London theatrical scene. Park Theatre has received five Olivier nominations, won Offie Awards for Best New Play, Best Set Design and Best Foodie Experience, and won The Stage's Fringe Theatre of the Year and Accessible Theatre Award.

Park Theatre is an inviting and accessible venue, delivering work of exceptional calibre in the heart of Finsbury Park. We work with writers, directors and designers of the highest quality to present compelling, exciting and beautifully told stories across our two intimate spaces.

Our programme encompasses a broad range of work from classics to revivals with a healthy dose of new writing, producing in-house as well as working in partnership with emerging and established producers. We strive to play our part within the UK's theatre ecology by offering mentoring, support and opportunities to artists and producers within a professional theatre-making environment.

Our Creative Learning strategy seeks to widen the number and range of people who participate in theatre, and provides opportunities for those with little or no prior contact with the arts.

In everything we do we aim to be warm and inclusive; a safe, welcoming and wonderful space in which to work, create and visit.

★★★★★ *"A five-star neighbourhood theatre."* Independent

As a registered charity [number 1137223] with no regular public subsidy, we rely on the kind support of our donors and volunteers. To find out how you can get involved visit parktheatre.co.uk

For Park Theatre

Artistic Director	Jez Bond
Executive Director	Rachael Williams
Community Engagement Manager	Nina Graveney-Edwards
Access Coordinator	Sarah Howard
Creative Learning Leader	Amy Allen
Development Director	Tania Dunn
Development Manager	Katie Munns
Finance Director	Elaine Lavelle
Finance & Administration Officer	Nicola Brown
General Manager	Rosie Preston
Producer Programmer	Daniel Cooper
Administrator	Mariah Sayer
Duty Venue Managers	Barry Card, Natasha Green, Shaun Joynson
Head of Hospitality	Diogo Silva
Restaurant Assistant Manager	James Dathorne
Pizza Chef	Marco Mezzelani
Sales & Marketing Director	Dawn James
Sales & Ticketing Manager	Matthew Barker
Marketing Manager	Mary Chafer
Senior Box Office Supervisor	Natasha Green
Box Office Supervisors	Greg Barnes & Jack Mosedale
Public Relations for Mobius Industries	Emma Berge
Technical & Buildings Manager	Sacha Queiroz
Deputy Technical & Buildings Manager	Neal Gray
Apprentice Buildings Technician	Teddy Nash

Trustees:
Kurt Barling, Hedda Beeby, Andrew Cleland-Bogle, Robert Hingley, Mars Lord, Bharat Mehta, Rufus Olins, Nigel Pantling (Chair), Victoria Phillips, Jo Parker, Julia Tyrrell

Associate Artist	Mark Cameron
Creative Director Emeritus	Melli Marie
Founding President	Jeremy Bond † (1939–2020)

With thanks to all of our supporters, donors and volunteers.

THEATRE UNLOCKED was formed in 2017 by Elis Shotton and Catherine Cranfield, after a discussion about theatre, in a central Manchester pub.

In early 2018, **FLUSHED** became the first project of Theatre Unlocked, premiering at 53two, in Manchester, and becoming the first recipient of their 'FOUNDation' award. **FLUSHED** went on to perform at multiple theatres and play to sold out audiences, receiving multiple 5-star reviews and winning Voice Magazine's 2018 'Pick of the Fringe' award.

In 2019 Theatre Unlocked produced *Zucchini*, a play that was written by Elis and supported by funding from Arts Council England. The show was met with critical acclaim and multiple 5-star reviews.

The success of these productions has paved the way for Theatre Unlocked to continue their creative endeavors, and to collaborate with other venues and artists to produce urgent, exciting, and thought-provoking work.

Theatre Unlocked is a company limited by guarantee.
Registered company no: 11649930

www.theatreunlocked.co.uk

About Grace Dickson Productions

Founded during the 2020 Coronavirus pandemic, Grace Dickson Productions encompasses the independent producing work of Grace Dickson, the company's Executive Director & Creative Producer.

Grace Dickson Productions is a company that develops and produces formally innovative & bitingly relevant new writing, that champions marginalised voices. GDP works collaboratively with artists on professional development, as well as creating work that isn't afraid to make a noise and ruffle some feathers.

GDP endeavours to produce imaginative, playful, and boundary-breaking work, that represents the world we live in and the worlds beyond it.

GDP's producing credits include *Flushed* by Catherine Cranfield (with Theatre Unlocked & Park Theatre), *Belly Up* by Julia Grogan & Lydia Higman (with Daring Hare Productions), *Different Owners at Sunrise* by Laurie Ogden, and *Catching Comets* by Piers Black (with Ransack Theatre).

CAST

ELIZABETH HAMMERTON | *Marnie*
Elizabeth is an award-winning actor from London, who trained at LAMDA. She read Drama at The University of Manchester and graduated with a BA in 2017. *Flushed* at Park Theatre marks Elizabeth's professional stage debut. TV credits include: *Pandora* (The CW).

IONA CHAMPAIN | *Jen*
Iona is an award-winning and BAFTA nominated actor from Suffolk, who trained with the National Youth Theatre. She read Drama at The University of Manchester and graduated with a BA in 2018. Theatre credits include: *Flushed* (Park Theatre, Barbican Centre, Fertility Fest, Underbelly Edinburgh); *Black Fate* (The Beacon); *Gateways* (Redgates Theatre). TV credits include: *The Third Day: Autumn* (Sky Atlantic).

CREATIVE TEAM

CATHERINE CRANFIELD | *Writer & Director*
Catherine is an award-winning writer and director from Hampshire, who trained at Mountview Academy of Theatre Arts, graduating with an MA in Theatre Directing in 2019. She read Drama at The University of Manchester and graduated with a BA in 2017. Theatre credits include: *Flushed* (Park Theatre, Barbican Centre, Fertility Fest, Underbelly Edinburgh, 53two); *The Net Kill* (Clapham Omnibus, Brighton Fringe); *Dogs of Society* (Golden Goose Theatre); *Island Town* (Catalyst Festival Mountview).

ELIS SHOTTON | *Executive Producer*
Elis is an award-winning writer and producer from Chester, who trained at the Royal Central School of Speech and Drama, graduating with an MA in Writing in 2020. He read Drama at The University of Manchester and graduated with a BA in 2017. Theatre credits include: *Flushed* (Park Theatre, Barbican Centre, Fertility Fest, Underbelly Edinburgh, 53two); *A Different Tune* (The Brewery Arts Centre); *Zucchini* (53two).

GRACE DICKSON | *Associate Producer*
Grace is an award-winning producer from Newcastle, who trained at Mountview Academy of Theatre Arts, graduating with an MA in Creative Producing in 2019. She read Mathematics at The University of Edinburgh and graduated with a BSc in 2018. Credits include: Company Producer for Grace Dickson Productions, THESE GIRLS, and Lagahoo Productions. Associate Producer for Archipelago and Conflicted Theatre. Assistant Producer to Ellie Caughton for LUNG, Breach, and Barrel Organ. General Manager for Rhum and Clay.

ANTHONY ENGLEZOU | *Lighting Design*
Anthony is a lighting designer from London, who trained at Mountview Academy of Theatre Arts. Theatre credits include: *Flushed* (Park Theatre); *Badgers Can't Be Friends* (Southwark Playhouse, King's Head Theatre, Catalyst Festival Mountview).

OSCAR MAGUIRE | *Sound Design*
Oscar is a multidisciplinary designer from London. He studied Architecture at the Bartlett School of Architecture UCL and graduated with a BSc in 2018. Theatre credits include: *Flushed* (Park Theatre); *Speed Dial* (Vault Festival); *Murder on the*

Dance Floor (Pleasance Courtyard Edinburgh); *Tobacco Road* (Pleasance Courtyard Edinburgh); *Woyzeck* (Pleasance Dome Edinburgh).

ALICE WOOD | *Stage Manager*
Alice is a London based stage manager, who trained at LAMDA. Theatre credits include: *When Darkness Falls* (Park Theatre); *Gentlemen Prefer Blondes* (Union Theatre); *West End Does: The Magic of Animation 2* (Cadogan Hall); *Market Boy* (Union Theatre); *Doctor Faustus* (Sam Wanamaker Playhouse, Globe Theatre); *West End Bares: Top Off The Pops* (Shaftesbury Theatre); *Motown the Musical* (Shaftesbury Theatre).

For further information on Premature Ovarian Insuffiency, please visit **The Daisy Network**'s website – organisation dedicated to supporting those affected by POI.

www.daisynetwork.org
Twitter: @thedaisynet
Instagram: @thedaisynetwork
Facebook: @DaisyNetwork

For Jane and Michael Cranfield

Flushed

By Catherine Cranfield

Characters

MARNIE and **JEN** – two sisters in their early twenties.

FLUSHED is written to be performed on a simple stage. The set should only consist of two toilets, but tiles or vinyl flooring may also be used to support the bathroom aesthetic. There should be no additional scenery, no furniture, no props, no explicit mime, and no costume changes.

When a toilet lid is up, that loo should be acknowledged as existing in the bathroom that the characters are currently in. By the same token, when a toilet lid is down, that loo should not be acknowledged. The positioning of lids should take place during scene transitions, which may also be supported by a pink lighting state. Both actors should remain on stage for the duration of the performance. Each scene takes place in a bathroom.

A forward slash mark (/) marks the point of interruption in overlapping dialogue.

A dash (-) marks a point of interruption.

A comma on a separate line (,) indicates a pause, a rest, a shift, or a silence, the length of which should be determined by the context.

An asterisk (*) marks the passage of time, the length of which should be determined by the context.

The absence of a full stop at the end of a line, or an ellipsis, indicates an interruption of thought or a trailing off.

*Lights up on **MARNIE** and **JEN**, sat on the toilet in neighbouring cubicles, in the bathroom of a fancy restaurant.*

MARNIE Oh fuck.

JEN What?

MARNIE No no no for fuck's / sake.

JEN What?

MARNIE I dropped it.

JEN Dropped what?

MARNIE My tampon.

JEN Oh fuck.

MARNIE Fuck.

JEN So it's really –

MARNIE Yes.

JEN And you've not got –

MARNIE No.

JEN Well hold on I might have something.

***JEN** checks her bag.*

MARNIE Anything?

JEN No.

MARNIE Owh. This is bad, this is very very bad.

JEN Can't you just

MARNIE Can't I just what?

JEN You know. Fish it out.

MARNIE Fish. It. Out?

JEN I was just suggesting.

MARNIE It's sodden.

JEN Alright.

MARNIE Have you ever used a tampon?

JEN Alright, sorry! Look let's just ask someone.

MARNIE Who?

JEN DOES ANYBODY HAVE A SPARE TAMPON?

MARNIE SHHH!

JEN What?

MARNIE Stop shouting!

JEN I was just checking.

MARNIE Well *just* don't.

JEN Alright.

,

MARNIE How long have we been in here?

JEN	Dunno. Five minutes maybe?
MARNIE	Oh god.
JEN	Marnie.
MARNIE	You know what they're gonna think.
JEN	Don't be ridiculous.
MARNIE	They will.
JEN	Who cares?
MARNIE	I care.
JEN	Girls poo.
MARNIE	Not on first dates they don't.
JEN	Well this one does. If a gals gotta go a gals gotta go.
MARNIE	Can we get back to the situation please?
JEN	Sorry. Right. How bad is it?
MARNIE	It's bad.
JEN	Can't you just toilet roll?
MARNIE	It's like Niagara Falls down there.
JEN	Day two?
MARNIE	Day two.
JEN	Bummer.

MARNIE   Fuck it. It's just gonna have to work for now.

JEN   You've got this.

                MARNIE begins to wrap the loo roll around her underwear.

MARNIE   I don't know if it's gonna

                I mean these aren't exactly the easiest underwear to

JEN   Just keep rolling it round.

MARNIE   Yeah fine just, bear with me.

                Right, okay I think that's

                Alright. I'm good.

JEN   How long do you reckon you've got?

MARNIE   I'd say an hour tops?

JEN   Doable.

MARNIE   We'd better get back.

JEN   Marnie?

MARNIE   Yeah?

JEN   How're you feeling about the whole *George Michael* situation?

MARNIE   Situation? He's dead isn't / he?

JEN No. Out there.

MARNIE Oh my god.

Truth?

JEN Truth.

MARNIE It's kind of like watching paint dry.

JEN Oh thank God.

MARNIE I mean George *and* Michael that's

JEN I know.

MARNIE They should never double date.

JEN Never.

MARNIE And their chat is just

JEN Painful.

MARNIE I mean I don't want to be dramatic but I think I'd have more fun taking a cheese grater to my face.

JEN What a pleasant image.

MARNIE He's a train *station* spotter. I mean I'm sorry can we just take a moment?

JEN What even is that?

MARNIE Lord only knows.

JEN God. I need a cigarette.

MARNIE Jen.

JEN This is my first one all week.

MARNIE Well that's a lie.

JEN It is not.

MARNIE I saw you have one two days ago.

JEN Where?

MARNIE You were literally sat on our doorstep having a cigarette.

JEN Yes but that was a menthol.

MARNIE So?

JEN So it's basically a breath mint.

MARNIE That's some interesting logic you've got there.

JEN Yeah. Well. Shut up.

MARNIE Fine.

,

JEN We have been in here a while haven't we.

MARNIE Maybe something happened to us.

JEN Maybe you got food poisoning…

MARNIE Maybe it was the clams…

JEN	They did look a bit dodgy.
MARNIE	Did they?
JEN	No.
MARNIE	Shit. Sorry.
JEN	Listen, all I'm saying is that a swift exit might just be an inevitable occurrence.
MARNIE	But we can't just
	I mean could we just
	leave…
JEN	Marnie! / No!
MARNIE	Sorry, bad / idea.
JEN	Could we?
MARNIE	I mean we could.
JEN	We could.
MARNIE	We really really could.
JEN	We could just walk straight out of here go home get some wine.
MARNIE	Get a tampon.
JEN	Get a tampon get some wine.
MARNIE	You already said wine.

JEN	I'd *really* like some wine.
MARNIE	What if they see us?
JEN	They won't see us.
	(sung) Just gotta have faith, faith, faith.
MARNIE	Please stop.
JEN	I am on fire today.

.

MARNIE	Okay, so how do we go about this?

*

MARNIE and JEN are doing their make-up at home, in the bathroom mirror.

JEN	Have you messaged him?
MARNIE	Who?
JEN	Who? Martin fucking Freeman who'd you think?
MARNIE	No.
JEN	Good girl.
MARNIE	He messaged me.
JEN	Interesting. And what did this message entail?

MARNIE   Nothing exciting. Just asked if I was going tonight.

JEN   And you said...

MARNIE   Yeah.

JEN   *Yeah?* Bandanna-Dan asks if you're going tonight and all you can say is *yeah?*

MARNIE   I put two kisses.

JEN   Did he reply?

MARNIE   Not yet.

JEN   Not yet? What's he gonna reply to *yeah?* Chill. Sick. Awesome.

MARNIE   I don't know. See you later?

JEN   Wow. Your conversations sound riveting.

MARNIE   Don't make this a thing Jen. This is not a thing.

JEN   Okay.

              I mean it could be a -

MARNIE   Jen this discussion isn't happening.

              ,

              How are my flicks?

JEN checks MARNIE's eyeliner.

JEN   Left's bigger.

MARNIE   Can you just

JEN   Hold on.

JEN fixes MARNIE's eyeliner.

There you go.

MARNIE   Thanks.

,

Have I fucked it?

JEN   It's fine I fixed it.

MARNIE   No with

JEN   Oh so this *is* up for discussion?

MARNIE   Not discussion just

conversation.

JEN   Well *conversationally* I would suggest that you have not at all fucked it. I mean it can only be a good sign that he messaged you in the first place, right?

MARNIE   Do you think?

JEN   Hundred percent.

,

Listen, on another note.

MARNIE Yeah?

JEN Have you had any thoughts about Dad's birthday?

MARNIE Dad's birthday?

JEN Yeah.

MARNIE Dad's birthday that's tomorrow?

JEN That's the one yeah.

MARNIE Funnily enough it had crossed my mind.

JEN Have you got him anything or

MARNIE Well I was gonna run some flowers over in the morning.

JEN Right.

Cool.

Any chance I can get in on that?

MARNIE What on *my* flowers? No.

JEN Please Marns. I was gonna get him a Moonpig but I'm just a bit strapped for cash.

MARNIE They're like three pounds Jen. You've got to get a proper job.

JEN Acting is a proper job.

MARNIE One that pays you *money*.

JEN It can it does I did that advert.

MARNIE Which advert?

JEN That PPI advert with the singing duck and the catchy jingle.

MARNIE That was last October. And it was shit.

JEN Look it's just a bit

difficult.

At the moment.

MARNIE Listen, Jen. You're my little sister you're my best friend and I love having you live with me I really do and, and I'm more than happy to support you but you've got / to start

JEN Look I've got an audition in a couple of days, okay? And I've actually got a really good feeling about it.

MARNIE Fine just

fine.

But you're taking the flowers round in the morning.

*

MARNIE and JEN are in the bathroom at a house party. JEN is vomiting and MARNIE is looking after her.

MARNIE   OCCUPIED!

It's alright Jenny it's okay.

JEN   I'm so sorry I didn't mean to

JEN vomits.

MARNIE   There we go it's okay babe it's okay.

JEN   I'm not

JEN vomits.

MARNIE   That's it. Get it all out. That's it.

IT'S ENGAGED!

JEN burps.

Better?

JEN   I think so.

MARNIE   Do you need to go again?

JEN leans over the loo seat to check if she does.

JEN   No.

MARNIE   Alright love, now can you stand up?

JEN   Yeah.

JEN tries to stand up. She can't.

Woah-kay no sit down.

You're a fucking liability, do you know that?

JEN I'm sorry Marnie I'm just really fucking

I'm just really very

I'm really very sorry.

MARNIE It's alright / hun.

JEN I'm so sorry Marnie!

MARNIE You mentioned.

JEN And the thing is

the thing is. I don't even know this, when this became a situation or, or when the situation became about because I was fine, I was so fine and then

JEN gags.

and then

JEN vomits.

MARNIE Okay. There we go.

Oh for fuck's sake. IT'S ENGAGED!!

JEN takes a moment.

JEN	I'm good.
MARNIE	You're good?
JEN	Yes. Very very sorry.
MARNIE	Shall we head home?
JEN	No. No no no no no you should stay you should
MARNIE	You need some sleep.
JEN	*You* need to speak to Dan.
MARNIE	I've already spoken to Dan.
JEN	When?
MARNIE	It's fine, I spoke to him.
JEN	Have you spoken to him?
MARNIE	Yes.
JEN	Where was I?
MARNIE	You were
	I spoke to him. Okay? So let's go.
JEN	Sleep?

*

MARNIE and JEN are in the bathroom at home. MARNIE is putting on face cream, whilst JEN spits out her mouth wash.

JEN	God. Bleurgh. That is vile.
MARNIE	What is? The mouthwash or the aftertaste of last night's vomit?
JEN	It's not a pleasant combination.
MARNIE	How are you feeling?
JEN	I feel like
	someone's sliced open my forehead, shat in it, and sewn it back up in a somewhat shoddy manner.
MARNIE	Delightful.
JEN	Owh. When did it go so wrong?
MARNIE	I *think* it was when you started pouring shots and chanting *tequila tequila tequila!*
JEN	Ow! Jesus. Can you not?
MARNIE	Sorry. Do you want some Nurofen?
JEN	I just took some.
	I didn't do anything embarrassing did I?
MARNIE	No. You're fine.
JEN	Thanks for looking after me.
MARNIE	It's okay.
JEN	I really am sorry.

MARNIE You mentioned.

JEN No I mean it, this is the last time.

MARNIE Okay babe.

JEN I mean it.

MARNIE I'm sure you do. I'm sure you're *never drinking again*.

JEN No. That would be ridiculous. I'm never drinking *tequila* again.

How was your night anyway?

MARNIE Good.

JEN Anything to report?

MARNIE Not really.

JEN Lies. You hooked up with Dan last night.

MARNIE How did you know?

JEN I didn't!

MARNIE / Oh for

JEN Tell me everything.

MARNIE There's nothing to tell.

JEN Lies! Slander! Poppycock!

MARNIE Poppycock?

JEN How was it?

MARNIE I wouldn't

I don't know.

JEN Well why not? He's perfect! Imagine the children, your chat, his cheekbones, how majestic it would be.

MARNIE I had to go home early.

JEN Oh god Marnie I'm so -

MARNIE If you say sorry one more time I swear to God.

JEN We can fix this.

MARNIE There's no need.

JEN Marnie I am not taking no for an answer text him / right now.

MARNIE I have.

JEN What?

MARNIE I texted him.

JEN And?

MARNIE *And* we're going for a drink next Friday.

JEN Where?

MARNIE Well we haven't decided yet.

JEN Well I never. Look at you arranging a date.

MARNIE It's not a date.

JEN It most certainly is a date and we need a game plan. What are you wearing?

MARNIE I mean I hadn't exactly –

JEN Marnie. This is incredibly important.

MARNIE But no pressure or anything. Yeah?

JEN Just the right amount of pressure. Now remember if the condom splits just let nature take its course cause he's a keeper.

*

MARNIE and JEN are in the bathroom at home. JEN is fake tanning her legs.

JEN But you had a good time?

MARNIE Sure.

JEN You didn't have a good time?

MARNIE No I did it was nice it was just a bit

I don't know. He was lovely, he was really really lovely and I was more than happy to go back to his but

JEN And how was that?

MARNIE	It was

fine. |
JEN	Fine?
MARNIE	Yeah.
JEN	Fine as in fireworks butterflies or fine as in —
MARNIE	Fine as in average at best?
JEN	Did he have a small willy?
MARNIE	No! Look it's

it's not like it was bad it wasn't *bad sex* it was just a bit

I don't know. Maybe I need to start sleeping with people I actually care about. Anything else is just

well to be perfectly honest anything else is just more work than a wank. |
| **JEN** | Take it you won't be seeing him again then? |
| **MARNIE** | I don't think so.

JEN inspects her legs. |
| **JEN** | Are these even? Have I missed any? |

MARNIE checks JEN's legs.

MARNIE	You're actually fine for once.
JEN	Woo! We should celebrate.
MARNIE	Celebrate?
JEN	Yes. Celebrate. You're done with Dan and I've never not missed any patches before.
MARNIE	Listen I'm not exactly
	What's wrong with Dan?
JEN	Nothing.
MARNIE	No go on what's wrong with Dan?
JEN	Nothing's *wrong* with Dan. You're the one who said he's boring.
MARNIE	I never said that.
JEN	Yes you did.
MARNIE	Well not *boring* just
	Times New Roman.
JEN	Times New Roman?
MARNIE	Yeah.
JEN	I see.
MARNIE	Yeah.
JEN	Right.

	Well then let's go out, let's get very drunk, and let's find you someone who's a bit more windings.
MARNIE	I mean as tempting as that offer is I'm not really feeling it / tonight.
JEN	*(Sung) You can dance! You can / jive!*
MARNIE	/ Jen I'm honestly knackered.
JEN	*(Sung) Having the time of your life! Ooo see that girl! Watch that scene! Digging the dancing / queen!*
MARNIE	Jenny / I'm serious.
JEN	*(Sung) Friday night and the lights are / low.*
MARNIE	Stop it!
JEN	Oh come on Marns! It's actually a Friday. And you still haven't changed the lightbulbs in here so the lights are reasonably low.
MARNIE	I'm tired Jen.
JEN	You're always tired.
MARINE	I am not!
JEN	Marnie. We owe this to Meryl.
MARNIE	You are aware that Meryl Streep didn't actually write Dancing / Queen?

JEN	*(Sung) You can / dance!*
MARNIE	Alright! Alright just, please, no more singing.
JEN	Deal.

,

MARNIE	How did that audition go by the way?
JEN	Hmm?
MARNIE	Your audition? The Dyson ad?
JEN	Oh, right, yeah. Didn't get it.

*

MARNIE and JEN are sat in neighbouring cubicles, in the club toilets.

MARNIE	CAN WE GO SOON?
JEN	WHAT?
MARNIE	CAN. WE. GO.
JEN	WE'VE ONLY BEEN HERE FIVE MINUTES.
MARNIE	I'M REALLY NOT FEELING IT.
JEN	WHY NOT?
MARNIE	BECAUSE I'M SOBER. AND BECAUSE THEY'RE PLAYING GARETH GATES.

JEN	I WILL BUY YOU A JAGER BOMB BUT I WILL NOT HEAR A BAD WORD SAID AGAINST GARETH GATES.
MARNIE	Why is there never any fucking loo roll?
	JEN, HAVE YOU GOT ANY LOO ROLL?
JEN	NO.
MARNIE	Brilliant.
JEN	JUST SWIFT IT.
MARNIE	SWIFT IT?
JEN	SHAKE IT OFF.

JEN stands up, 'shakes it off', and exits the cubicle.

	YOU NEARLY DONE?
MARNIE	TWO SECONDS.
JEN	HURRY UP I WANNA DANCE.
MARNIE	TWO. SECONDS.

MARNIE stands up, reluctantly 'shakes it off', and exits the cubicle.

	Jen I've got a headache.
JEN	Well let's get a drink and / then
MARNIE	No, Jen I want to leave.

JEN	It's half twelve.
MARNIE	I'm sorry I'm just a bit –
JEN	*Half twelve*, just

    Look. I'll buy you a drink, you'll feel better, and if you're still not feeling it we'll go home. Okay? Come here.

JEN fixes MARNIE's eyeliner.

    There we go. Much better.

MARNIE starts to cry.

    Hey, what's wrong?

MARNIE	I've got a headache.
JEN	Woah, come here.

They hug.

    Let's go home.

*

JEN has called MARNIE into the bathroom at home, to look at something.

JEN	Please Marnie.
MARNIE	No.
JEN	Please!
MARNIE	No!

JEN	Can't you just -
MARNIE	Absolutely not.

JEN makes a sad face.

	It's not happening.
JEN	But you have to.
MARNIE	I do not *have* to.
JEN	You're my sister.
MARNIE	Exactly. It's weird.
JEN	I'd do it for you.
MARNIE	That doesn't / mean
JEN	Please!
MARNIE	Oh God.
	Alright.
JEN	Thank you thank you thank you.

MARNIE inspects – briefly.

MARNIE	Yep.
JEN	*Yep?* What do you mean *yep?*
MARNIE	That's a vagina.
JEN	Yes I know it's a vagina it's my vagina what's wrong with it?

MARNIE	There's nothing wrong with it.
JEN	I'm telling you, something's not right.
MARNIE	You've got thrush babe. Or a UTI or
JEN	I've got herpes.
MARNIE	You're being ridiculous.
JEN	I am not.
MARNIE	You do not have herpes.
JEN	I mean I can deal with the clap It's not ideal but you can get rid of it you know but *herpes*
	that shit's for life.
MARNIE	Did you use protection?
JEN	Yeah.
MARNIE	Then what makes you think –
JEN	Runny nose, check, shivers, check, pain when passing urine, definitely check.
MARNIE	Jenny. How many times? Do not consult Doctor Google. You've got a cold.
JEN	I've got flu-like symptoms.
MARNIE	Right. I'm out.

JEN   No wait please. Can you just have another look?

MARNIE   No! Ask a real doctor.

JEN   I'm scared.

MARNIE   Jen. I promise you. You do not have herpes. Okay? Just go and get a check-up.

JEN   Okay.

MARNIE   Look I'll, I'll come with you actually. I need to get something looked at.

JEN   Everything okay?

MARNIE   Yeah. Yeah everything's fine it's just

Well I'm late so

JEN   What? How late?

MARNIE   I'm

I'm not really sure, I –

JEN   Have you done a test?

MARNIE   Yes.

JEN   And?

MARNIE   And it was negative.

JEN   And how long ago did you take it?

MARNIE   About a week ago?

JEN	And it was negative?
MARNIE	Yes. It was negative.
JEN	Well surely it's fine then?
MARNIE	Probably but
	Well my jeans don't fit me anymore.
JEN	Which ones?
MARNIE	Pretty much all of them.
JEN	Really? You can't tell.
MARNIE	*I* can tell. I'm fat and I'm late and / I'm actually
JEN	You are not fat don't be ridiculous.
	And you wouldn't be showing yet anyway so calm down. Look, let's just take another test. Okay?
MARNIE	Okay. Shit Jen what if it's
	I mean what if I'm actually –
JEN	You won't be. Okay? But it never hurts to check.

*

MARNIE and JEN are in the bathroom at home. MARNIE is taking a pregnancy test.

JEN	Well go on then.
MARNIE	I'm trying.
JEN	Just do it.
MARNIE	Stop distracting me!
JEN	It's just a wee!
MARNIE	Ssshhh!
JEN	Alright.

,

MARNIE	Got it.
JEN	Disco.
MARNIE	How long did it say?
JEN	Trois minutos.
MARNIE	Since when were you fluent in French and Spanish?
JEN	*Spench* if you will.
MARNIE	Go on then I will.
JEN	Alrighty then.

,

MARNIE Fuck.

Jen what if it's / actually

JEN   It won't be.

                  But *if* it is then

                  then you're going to be fine.

                              *

   MARNIE and JEN are in the bathroom at home.

MARNIE   How long's it been?

JEN   About two minutes.

MARNIE   Right.

                  Right. Okay. Talk to me.

JEN   About what?

MARNIE   Anything just say anything just

                  I don't know. What takes a minute?

                  ,

JEN   *(Sung) Every day when you're walking down the street. Everybody that you meet. Has an original point of view.*

MARNIE   Really?

JEN   *(Sung) And I say*

   JEN points at MARNIE.

                  hey.

MARNIE's response is reluctant... at first.

MARNIE   Hey.

JEN   *(Sung) What a wonderful kind of day.*

JEN	**MARNIE**
Where you can learn to work and play. And get along with each other.	Where you can learn to work and play. *(Sung) And get along with each other.*

MARNIE and JEN break into a fully choreographed dance routine.

You got to listen to your heart, listen to the beat, listen to the rhythm, the rhythm of the street, open up your eyes, open up your ears, get together and make things better, by working together.	*You got to listen to your heart, listen to the beat, listen to the rhythm, the rhythm of the street, open up your eyes, open up your ears, get together and make things better, by working together.*
It's a simple message. And it comes from the heart.	*It's a simple message. And it comes from the heart.*
If you believe / in yourself.	
	Believe in yourself.
Well that's the place / to start.	
	To start

And I say hey.

                            Hey!

What a wonderful kind of day.

                            Hey!

What a wonderful kind of day.

                            Hey!

What a wonderful kind of day.

                            Hey!

Hey! D.W

                            Hey!

Woahhhh!   *Woahhh!*

MARNIE   Wow.

JEN   Fuck yes.

,

MARNIE   What's it saying?

    JEN checks the pregnancy test. The result is negative.

JEN   You're all good.

MARNIE   Really?

JEN	Yep.
MARNIE	Really?
JEN	Yes. One blue line.
MARNIE	Oh. Well. Thank fuck for that.
JEN	I told you it would be fine.
MARNIE	Yeah.
JEN	Hold on. Are you disappointed?
MARNIE	What? No.
JEN	Yes you are you're disappointed.
MARNIE	I am not.
JEN	Did you want to be?
MARNIE	No!
	I mean
	would it have been so bad?
JEN	Oh my god.
MARNIE	No. Listen. Shut up, okay? I am relieved I am it's just
	well you know I've always wanted to and, and okay don't laugh but
	but I was in The White Company the other day and they had these little socks and they

	were just the most adorable little things and there were those like you know like Jellycats? Those stuffed animals? The really soft ones? Well there was this one white rabbit / and it had

JEN   You're twenty-five.

MARNIE   And?

JEN   *And* Bandanna-Dan is hardly daddy material.

MARNIE   Dan is a stand up guy. Okay? He's a doctor.

JEN   He's training.

MARNIE   To *become* a doctor.

JEN   Marnie.

MARNIE   I know. I know. I just

I just couldn't help myself from thinking

fuck.

You know like seriously *fuck*. There could actually be a tiny human just

growing.

inside me.

JEN   Bleurgh. God. It's just so

weird.

MARNIE Weird?

JEN Yeah. Just a tiny human growing inside ya, it's just a bit

MARNIE It's the most natural thing in the universe.

JEN Is it?

MARNIE What, you don't want kids?

JEN Well don't say it like that.

MARNIE Like what?

JEN Like I've just shot the Easter Bunny.

MARNIE Sorry I just

I didn't know.

JEN Look, it's not that I don't want kids I just don't

want

kids.

MARNIE Since when?

JEN I don't know. Since always? I guess I don't

I just don't have that maternal instinct. You know? And I'm not saying never I mean potentially one day yes of course I might you know I might meet someone and I might think yeah.

Yes. You know? Let's do it. Let's merge our DNA and make tiny combinations of ourselves but then that's a decision you know that's an active choice it's not just some imaginary little person that vomits and poos and screams and cries it's

What? Does that make me a bad person?

MARNIE   No. Maybe. I don't know.

JEN   Because it shouldn't.

MARNIE   No.

JEN   Anyway, future Jen can worry about all of that, and so can future Marnie.

MARNIE   Yeah.

JEN   And I promise you that one day I will be buying you all of the tiny socks and white rabbits.

MARNIE   Okay.

Listen I still

I think I'm still gonna get that check-up.

JEN   Why?

MARNIE   Well I mean I'm still late so

JEN   Okay. But Marns? You're all good.

*

MARNIE and JEN are on the phone to one another. MARNIE is sat on the loo at work and JEN is sat on the loo at home.

JEN	So there's this girl. Right? There's this little girl called

Marnie.

And she *loves* tractors, like, can't get enough of them, literally, everything she owns has like tractor prints on it, or is like, like it's like shaped like a tractor or, or, because she lives on a farm. Okay? She lives on a farm and she is just *obsessed* with tractors. Anyway. So. She grows up and she kind of moves on with her life, she starts smoking and drinking and don't get me wrong she still *likes* tractors but, well she's in with the cool kids now so they've sort of taken a backseat in her mind –

MARNIE	Where is this going?

JEN	Bear with me.

MARNIE	Right.

JEN	So she goes to uni. She gets the degree, she gets a first, she's gonna be a lawyer, everything is just *amazing*. And by this point, all that's left of her rural youth are fond memories of tractors past. Then one day she's working on this *huge* case. Massive. Groundbreaking. Hot shit. So she's working away and you know it's like June July it's pretty hot so she cracks open a window, you know as you do, and she's working working working and then BAM. In rushes this *huge* gust of wind, and it blows all of the papers everywhere, they're all over the room and there's just coffee everywhere and it's all completely fucked. Then. Her boss rocks up, or like, the woman she's working on the case with, and she totally flips out because this is bad, right? This is very bad news. But Marnie's chill. She's fine. She turns to her boss, super casual, and says don't worry, I've got this. And she takes a big breath in.

JEN breaths in, dramatically.

And as she does she sucks everything in, all of the coffee, all of the paper, everything, and then she breathes it all out again in one big *whoosh*.

JEN breathes out, dramatically.

And suddenly. As if by magic. Everything is back to normal. The coffee's the cups. The papers are stacked.

MARNIE   Jen I'm actually / quite

JEN	Ssshhh!
	The papers are stacked. And her boss just looks at her. And she's all, how the hell did you do that? And Marnie just smiles. Looks her dead in the eye and says
	I'm an *ex-tractor-fan*.
	,
MARNIE	Are you done?
JEN	Yes.
MARNIE	Well.
JEN	Well what?
MARNIE	Well it's
	I mean it's actually quite good to be fair.
JEN	Bloody brilliant I'd say.
MARNIE	Unnecessary build up.
JEN	Ah see that's where you're wrong the build up's the best bit. It's what distinguishes it from a cheap gag to a highly banterous rollercoaster of emotions.
MARNIE	Right. Lucky you caught me actually I'm just taking a five. One of the kids thought he could out-do Henry the Eighth and tried to marry every single girl in the class.

JEN	Amazing.
MARNIE	Yeah well it got a bit dramatic actually so the Head's giving them a talking to.
JEN	Alas.
MARNIE	So anyway can I help you with something or did you just ring to tell me that joke?
JEN	To enlighten you. Yes.
MARNIE	Well thank you I certainly feel enlightened.
JEN	You're welcome. Anytime.
MARNIE	Hang on I'm getting another call. Call you later?
JEN	Okay. / Bye.
MARNIE	Bye.

JEN hangs up the phone, and MARNIE answers the other call to hear her doctor on the other line.

MARNIE	Hello?
	Hi yes speaking.
	Oh hiya yeah not too bad thank you.
	Okay.
	Right. Well that's
	I mean that's good then.

I just don't quite erm

I mean what's going on with my periods?

I mean I'm a bit busy this week can't we just chat now?

Well I'm not exactly

Sorry what's going on?

Can you tell me what's going on please?

That sounds scary. Big words usually I mean that's not ideal is it big words from a doctor you know there's a reason a cold is just called a cold and that's erm sorry could you repeat that for me I'm not sure I

Right.

Shit.

Are you sure?

Right so I should, I should get a prescription or or or or something or

No I don't need options I, I need a prescription I need to fix this can't you just

Can I have kids?

*

MARNIE *is sat on the floor of the bathroom at home.* ***JEN*** *is stood outside the locked door.*

JEN	Can I come in?
	I made us some pasta. Well I tried to I sort of overcooked it and it tastes a bit like rubber. Not that I know what rubber tastes like. Obviously.
	Are you okay?
	Marnie?
MARNIE	Go away Jen.
JEN	What's wrong? You've been in there for ages.
MARNIE	Go. Away.
JEN	Just tell me what's wrong Marnie
	Right.
	Well.
	I'll just wait here then.

JEN sits down outside the door.

,

MARNIE	I had the chickenpox.
JEN	What?
MARNIE	When I was four. I had the chickenpox.
JEN	Yeah. I know.

MARNIE		Apparently there can be a link? It's rare but, but apparently there can be a link to chickenpox or or to malaria or tuberculosis even but I never had those I
		I had the chickenpox.
JEN		You're not making any
		A link to what?
MARNIE		I don't want to talk / about it.
JEN		A link to what Marnie?
		,
MARNIE		Premature Ovarian Insufficiency.
JEN		What?
MARNIE		Premature Menopause.
JEN		What are you
		Marnie can you please just open the door?
MARNIE		No.
JEN		Okay.
		So what you
		I mean I'm guessing you saw the doctor?
MARNIE		Yes.
		Look I'm sorry but can we not

	I'm just not / really
JEN	And they think it's that?
MARNIE	Yes.
JEN	Right.
	Are they sure?
MARNIE	I need more tests.
JEN	So they're not sure.
MARNIE	She seemed pretty certain.
JEN	Okay. So when are / the
MARNIE	In like five weeks or / so
JEN	And what kind of tests / are they?
MARNIE	Like blood tests I dunno. She wants me to get a few opinions.
JEN	So these other tests they're
MARNIE	Basically our FSH levels can fluctuate / so it's
JEN	FSH levels?
MARNIE	Follicle-stimulating hormone it's, it's what helps control our periods and the production of eggs.
JEN	/ Okay.

MARNIE And my levels are high they're, they're very high actually / and

JEN But they fluctuate?

MARNIE Please Jen.

JEN Sorry I'm just I'm trying to get my head around this just trying to think for a second just

Do they know why?

MARNIE No.

JEN So they don't know what's caused it?

MARNIE No.

JEN But they must know something.

MARNIE They don't.

JEN But that's

I mean that's insane that's

What and you think it's Chickenpox?

MARNIE Well I

I was on Google and –

JEN Doctor Google is a wanker.

	Look we're gonna sort this, okay? We are we just, we need to get confirmation before we panic and then –
MARNIE	It's been over a year.
JEN	What has?
MARNIE	I haven't had my period in over a year.
JEN	Really?
	Why didn't you
	But I've lent you tampons. I've made you hot water bottles I've
	Over a year are you serious?
	So you lied to me.
MARNIE	Jen this isn't about you.
JEN	Lied. To me. Your best friend.
MARNIE	My kid sister!
	,
	Sorry.
JEN	You should have told me.
MARNIE	I didn't
	I was terrified.
	When you're a kid and you start

When your body starts changing it's it's fucking scary but you know it's happening to everyone and there's information. Right? You're starting your period and your boobs are growing and it's weird but it's normal. Okay so this was like.

this was like it was happening all over again. My body was changing and it was just as scary but I knew it wasn't normal.

I was fucking terrified.

JEN I just wish I'd known I could have –

MARNIE You could have what Jen?

JEN I don't know seen a doctor or

MARNIE I didn't want to see a doctor. I didn't want to know what was happening.

JEN What you really had no idea?

MARNIE I knew that I couldn't sleep and I knew that I felt angry and anxious and tired but I never / thought

JEN So why didn't you see a doctor then?

MARNIE I don't know.

The other night I was trying to get to sleep and I was just *sweating*. So I had a shower and I just sort of sat there. Crying. Pretty

	tragic actually. Anyway I knew it was only getting worse so I
JEN	Listen if you take those tests and it's
	Then what?
MARNIE	If I take those tests and it *is* then
	then I can't have a baby.
JEN	What? There must be a chance?
MARNIE	It depends how far along / the whole
JEN	So there is / a chance?
MARNIE	There's not a chance Jen. It's too late there's not a fucking chance.
JEN	Yes! Yes there is Marnie you hear tonnes of stories people who can't have kids and stop trying and then they get pregnant it / happens.
MARNIE	Stop it.
JEN	Sally. Mum's friend. Remember? She was trying for years and then / one day
MARNIE	/ Stop.
JEN	one day she got / pregnant.
MARNIE	Please Jen stop!
	This is different.

,

JEN   Is it genetic?

MARNIE   What?

JEN   Is it genetic?

MARNIE   Really?

JEN   Sorry I just mean should I be getting tested too or –

MARNIE   Fuck you Jen.

JEN   What?

MARNIE   I can't have kids. Me. Do you understand that? I cannot have children don't ask me if it's genetic.

JEN   Marnie if it is I need to know I need to get tested.

MARNIE   So get tested! Don't ask me just do it!

JEN   Alright I

Sorry.

,

Hey at least you won't get fat.

MARNIE   What?

JEN   I was I'm sorry that was so stupid / I'm

MARNIE   Are you serious? I want to / get fat.

JEN   I know I'm sorry I'm just not / thinking

MARNIE   I want to get fat Jen.

I want people to look at me in the first few weeks and wonder, is she? And I want people to be too afraid to ask, you know in case I'd just indulged too much at Christmas.

I think I'd tease people you know? Make someone feel really bad.
They'd congratulate me and I could just start crying or act really offended or something. I reckon that could be quite fun. And then, when I'd start showing properly and it wouldn't be a question anymore that's when I'd have the *real* fun. I'd skip the queue for stuff like

like the loos at the theatre or

or Pizza Express.

I want to eat gherkins dipped in peanut butter and bagels coated in yogurt just because I can and

and I want to go to the hospital. And have all the check-ups even the scary ones. I want to be the first person in the world to hear their heartbeat. I want to feel them kick. I want to feel so terrified and so excited that I could just burst and, and I'd tell myself I could do it and I'd worry that I can't but I'd try my best anyway.

I want to watch them turn pink. I want the relief when you hear them cry and, and I want to hear the doctor say it's a boy, or it's a girl. And I want to hold that little boy or that little girl between my elbow and the palm of my hand and carry them to the window and say *hey*. Hey that's a tree. Out there. That's a tennis court. That's a car park that's a Ford fucking Focus that's

that's the world. You've arrived. We made it.

,

Yes.

JEN   Yes what?

MARNIE   Yes it can be genetic.

                         *

MARNIE and JEN are on the phone to one another. MARNIE is sat on the loo at home and JEN is at work.

MARNIE   Have you heard yet?

JEN   I have, yeah. Everything's normal so I'm

	I'm fine.
MARNIE	Good that's
	that's good.
JEN	Are you -
MARNIE	I'm fine no that's good that's I'm happy / for you.
JEN	I'm so sorry Marns.
MARNIE	No. No don't be.

MARNIE looks for some loo roll.

	God dammit why is there never any fucking loo roll?
JEN	What?
MARNIE	Nothing I'm
JEN	Marnie are you okay?
MARNIE	Yes! Yes. I'm fine. Listen I've got to erm
	I'll see you later.
JEN	Sure. Yeah okay. Love you.

*

JEN has been smoking in the bathroom at home and is attempting to waft the smell of smoke out of the window.

MARNIE is waiting outside the door to use the bathroom.

MARNIE   Are you nearly done in there?

JEN   Fuck shit.

Two seconds!

MARNIE   What are you doing in there?

JEN   Just give me

Just one minute!

JEN takes a final sniff, nods, and then opens the door.

Sorry. All done. You might wanna give it a minute.

MARNIE   It's fine I'm bursting.

MARNIE tries to enter the bathroom. JEN remains stood in the doorway, blocking the entrance.

JEN   Mhm. Sure.

MARNIE   Are you gonna let me in?

JEN   Yes. Of course.

JEN slowly steps out of the way.

After you.

MARNIE   Thank you?

MARNIE enters and smells the smoke immediately.

	Jen!
JEN	Yes?
MARNIE	Have you been smoking in here?
JEN	No?
MARNIE	Jenny!
JEN	I'm sorry!
MARNIE	We agreed!
JEN	It was only one.
MARNIE	If you want to smoke then do it outside!
JEN	Alright! I'm / sorry!
MARNIE	Not / inside!
JEN	It's pouring outside!
MARNIE	Really Jenny? In the bathroom?
JEN	I didn't want my room to smell.
MARNIE	What so you stink out the bathroom instead? Oh right yeah / that's fair.
JEN	/ I just
MARNIE	What happened to I'm quitting?
JEN	I am quitting.
MARNIE	Clearly.

JEN	I am quitting I just
	Rome wasn't built in a day.
MARNIE	Oh for God's sake.
JEN	Don't judge me!
MARNIE	I'm not.
JEN	You are!
MARNIE	Well can you blame me? How many times have you promised me? If you want to smoke then smoke but don't promise me you're done when / you're not.
JEN	I am!
MARNIE	You're not! You're not you're kidding yourself!
JEN	This is my first cigarette in three days.
MARNIE	Oh. Well. Congratu-fucking-lations have a medal.
JEN	Why are you being like this? I'm trying.
MARNIE	You're trying?
JEN	Yes!
MARNIE	Grow up Jen.
JEN	Grow up?

MARNIE   Yes actually yes grow up!

JEN   Alright *mum* pipe down.

           ,

           Shit. Marnie I / didn't

MARNIE   I have to pee.

JEN   Please Marns I didn't / mean

MARNIE   Get out!

JEN   Marnie I just want to help I just want to talk to you.

MARNIE   The doctor called earlier. They were right before. The tests? They were right.

JEN   Fuck.

MARNIE   Yep. It's official. I am barren I am broken I am –

JEN   Come on Marns you're being -

MARNIE   What Jen? What exactly am I being? It's the one thing that every woman should be able to do / and I can't.

JEN   / Fucking hell Marnie that's a bit

MARNIE   And they don't know why they don't know how come no one knows they just pass you around like some fucking hot potato until

	finally someone sits you down and says I'm really sorry.
	They're *sorry*.
	It's not fair.
JEN	I know.
MARNIE	No. No you don't know how could you you don't even
	I feel like I'm fifty. Twenty-five years old and I'm all
	shrivelled up.
	It's embarrassing.
JEN	You shouldn't be –
MARNIE	Don't. Okay don't do that don't tell me what I *should* or *shouldn't* be just
	Just get out.

*

MARNIE and JEN each sit down on the toilet. A transitional montage of reflection ensues. The transition should have no dialogue and should not exist within any one specific time or location, but rather it should act as an abstract bridge. In the original production this was supported by music and a pink lighting state. The simpler the better.

*

MARNIE and *JEN* are stood by the bathtub at home. *MARNIE* checks the water temperature.

JEN How's that?

MARNIE Jesus!

Hot.

JEN Shit sorry.

MARNIE It's fine I'll just give it a minute.

,

This is amazing. Is that a three wick candle?

JEN Frosted lavender.

MARNIE Very fancy.

JEN And the bubbles have a hint of jasmine.

MARNIE Nice. And how did you afford all of this may I ask?

JEN Well I

I got a job.

MARNIE What?

JEN Well a part really I, I got a part.

MARNIE Wait you got a part?

JEN Yeah.

MARNIE		Why didn't you tell me? A part in what?
JEN		Casualty.
MARNIE		Seriously?
JEN		Seriously.
MARNIE		Fuck! Congratulations that's amazing!
JEN		Thanks.
MARNIE		Wait so tell me everything?
JEN		Well it's you know it's early days yet so erm, anyway I'm gonna leave you to it.
MARNIE		Thank you.
JEN		It's just a bath.
MARNIE		No I mean

thank you.

Look Jen, I know I've not exactly been the easiest person to be around lately / and I |
| **JEN** | | Marnie you don't / need to |
| **MARNIE** | | Yes I do. I know you were only trying to help I was just so

I just wanted someone to tell me what to do and tell me how to react because I had no idea and then you tried and |

	and I wasn't fair on you. And I'm really sorry.
JEN	Well no. You weren't. But no part of this is exactly fair is it?
	And you're right. I should grow up.
MARNIE	Jenny I was / being
JEN	No I should. And I am. I bought a three wick candle for fuck's sake.
MARNIE	Well it doesn't get more grown up than that. Careful though cause I could get used to this.
JEN	Okay.
	,
	So how was the doctor today?
MARNIE	Fine yeah. I'm seeing someone else now so —
JEN	What? Again?
MARNIE	Yeah some specialist apparently. Anyway she's changed my pill so hopefully that's gonna help.
JEN	That's it?
MARNIE	For now. I mean there'll be HRT in the / future but

JEN	H R what now?
MARNIE	Sorry, erm, hormone replacement therapy.
JEN	That's good right?
MARNIE	Yeah.
	Yeah.
JEN	But for now what you're just, on the pill?
MARNIE	Yeah it's a, one step at a time, sort of thing.
JEN	Cool.
	Cool erm listen I've, I've been doing some thinking, well, you know, a lot of thinking, actually, and erm, I've been reading quite a lot and
	I mean have you thought about options?
MARNIE	Jen I really don't –
JEN	Obviously not now but like, in the future, have you thought about options?
MARNIE	Yes.
JEN	Because obviously I mean you'll work it out you know when the time comes you'll know what to do but
	but I have got cracking eggs.
MARNIE	Pun intended?

JEN	Always.
MARNIE	That's sweet Jen but / you don't
JEN	No I'm serious that's an actual thing you / can actually
MARNIE	Don't even go there.
JEN	Why not?
MARNIE	Because.
JEN	Because why?
MARNIE	Because because you're my sister and –
JEN	And what? I'd do it I want to.
MARNIE	Seriously?
JEN	Obviously.
MARNIE	That's I mean not now
JEN	Whenever. Okay? We can talk about it whenever it's just, it's on the table it's just chilling you can pick it up you can leave it whatever / you
MARNIE	I fucking love you.

JEN Love you more.

Do you want to know what I think?

MARNIE What's that then?

JEN I think that right now, you do you. You go out, you get fucked up, you make some stupid fucking horrific mistakes because you're twenty five years old and you can. And I think that one day *you're* going to want a baby.

MARNIE Jen.

JEN No you are. Because you always have. Remember when we were kids and we'd play pretend? You were always the mum because you'd call it. Shotgun! And you smashed it every time because you just are one.

MARNIE Jen / stop.

JEN You are! You look after me all the time you

you are you're a mum.

You've been dealt a shit hand and I'm so sorry because you're the last person in the world who

One day you're gonna want a baby, okay? And when that day comes you're gonna adopt or or foster or take my fucking eggs.

>   Or I mean you could take someone else's but you should probably take mine because

JEN gestures to herself.

>   Am I right?

MARNIE   You're not wrong.

JEN   Is the correct answer.

>   And whatever happens you're gonna be that baby's mum. Because you're gonna change it's nappies and you're gonna stay up all night whilst it cries or or because they've gone out and you can't sleep until they're home and
>
>   and you're not gonna miss out. On any of it. It's all there it's waiting for you it's going to happen, but you know what? Right now? Fuck it. I mean cry and be sad and take all the time that you need and I'm here. Right? I promise you I am *always* here.
>
>   But just say fuck it.

MARNIE   The water's gonna be

JEN   Say it!

>   ,

MARNIE   Fuck it

*

MARNIE and JEN are both sat on the toilet, in neighbouring cubicles, in the bathroom of a fun restaurant.

MARNIE Oh come on he's not that bad.

JEN He is that bad. He buys red milk.

MARNIE You're too fussy.

JEN Oh I'm sorry says *you*. However, I do think we may have finally hit the jackpot with your guy.

MARNIE Do you think we'll ever go on a double date where *both* people are socially acceptable human beings?

JENNY Probably not.

MARNIE No.

He is alright though isn't he?

JEN He is more than alright. And he can't take his eyes off you.

MARNIE Shut up.

He's very nice.

JEN But?

MARNIE Nothing he is he's lovely.

JEN	He's lovely but…
MARNIE	Nothing.
	Nothing it's just
	okay this might sound stupid or whatever but
	I mean when do I tell him?
JEN	Tell him what?
MARNIE	When do I tell him I can't have kids?
JEN	Well not now it's your first date!
MARNIE	No obviously not now but when? There's not exactly a good time to –
JEN	You're overthinking it.
MARNIE	I am not overthinking it.
JEN	Yes you are. Look just
	You're having a good time. Yes?
MARNIE	Yes.
JEN	So have a good time. You don't need to tell him anything.
MARNIE	I will do though. At some point. If not him then someone else who

	I mean what if I meet someone who's perfect? Well not perfect but perfect for *me*. You know? What if I fall in love with someone and they want kids?
JEN	You can still have kids.
MARNIE	You know what I mean.
JEN	No Marnie, you're not doing this.
MARNIE	Doing what?

JEN gets up, flushes the loo, and goes to wash her hands

JEN	You are not dismissing every single person who might potentially possibly probably actually like you because you're scared.
MARNIE	I'm not scared I'm being realistic. It's different for me having a baby it's not as easy.
JEN	Easy?
MARNIE	Yes.
JEN	You think pregnancy is easy?
MARNIE	No not easy just

Yes actually yes easy easier at least I mean there's no no forms or or or checks or rules or –

JEN You're panicking.

MARNIE I'm not / I'm just

JEN Stop / panicking.

MARNIE Okay / I'm just

JEN Why are you panicking?

MARNIE I'm panicking because

I'm panicking because I feel like at some point I could end up holding someone back.

,

JEN Have you ever considered that your plan B might be someone else's plan A?

MARNIE What do you mean?

JEN I mean not everyone wants kids.

MARNIE I know that.

JEN Some people aren't on board the baby train at all and that's fine that's more than / fine that's

MARNIE I know that I

I know.

	It would just be nice to have the option.
JEN	I know.
	But listen there's no need to rush anything. Okay? You're still young.
MARNIE	When did you get so wise?
JEN	I am actually incredibly intelligent.
MARNIE	Is that right?
JEN	Oh yes. Are you nearly ready?
MARNIE	Yep ready just
	two seconds.
JEN	What are you doing in there?
MARNIE	Just give me a minute.
JEN	Oh my god.
MARNIE	Shut up.
JEN	Are you pooing?
MARNIE	Yes okay yes I am pooing.
JEN	Well I never. Look at you pooing on a first date I am so proud.
MARNIE	Jenny I swear to / God.
JEN	Hey, guess what.

MARNIE What?

JEN You should be proud too.

MARNIE Proud of what?

JEN I haven't smoked since the bathroom incident.

MARNIE Really?

JEN Mhm. Not a single one. On my life.

MARNIE Well would you look at us? Overcoming our deepest darkest demons.

JEN I know. The times they are a-changin' my friend. One minute you're sat on the sofa minding your own and the next Gary Barlow's in the Live Lounge singing Despacito.

MARNIE What?

JEN Sometimes my mind just goes there.

MARNIE You're so weird.

JEN That's why you love me.

MARNIE Is that right?

JEN It is yes.

MARNIE If you say so.

JEN I do.

MARNIE Okay.

JEN I do say so.

MARNIE Alright then.

JEN Good. Well I'm glad that's settled.

MARNIE gets up, flushes the loo, and goes to wash her hands.

How was it?

MARNIE It was actually quite a pleasant experience.

JEN Mmm. It can be. Right come on then. You ready?

MARNIE Ready. Let's do this.

Lights down. End